W9-BPL-017

Hairy Tarantulas

by Joelle Riley

PULL AHEAD BOOKS
Animals

Lerner Publications Company • Minneapolis

Lerner Publications Company
A division of Lerner Publishing Group, Inc.
241 First Avenue North
Minneapolis, MN 55401 U.S.A.

Website address: www.lernerbooks.com

Words in *italic* type are explained in a glossary on page 30.

Library of Congress Cataloging-in-Publication Data

Riley, Joelle.
  Hairy tarantulas / by Joelle Riley.
    p.   cm. — (Pull ahead books. Animals)
  Includes bibliographical references and index.
  ISBN: 978-0-8225-6702-8 (lib. bdg. : alk. paper)
  1. Tarantulas—Juvenile literature. I. Title.
QL458.42.T5R55 2008
595.4'4—dc22   2006101044

Manufactured in the United States of America
1 2 3 4 5 6 – JR – 13 12 11 10 09 08

What is this hairy animal?

This animal is a tarantula. Tarantulas are the biggest *spiders* in the world.

Some tarantulas are as big as
a dinner plate!

A tarantula has eight legs.

At the front of a tarantula's body are
two *pedipalps*. The spider uses the
pedipalps to hold its food.

A tarantula has lots of eyes.

It has two long, sharp teeth called
fangs. The fangs are hidden under
its body.

A tarantula
doesn't have
any bones.
Instead, it
has a tough
skin called an
exoskeleton.

The skin is covered with hairs.
Some of the hairs are tiny stingers.

A tarantula can kick the stingers at
enemies to scare them away.

Some tarantulas live in deserts.
Their homes are holes in the ground
called *burrows*.

Other tarantulas live in *rain forests*.
Their homes are tube-shaped webs
high in the trees.

Tarantulas are shy. They spend most of their time hiding in their burrow or tube web.

At night, tarantulas hunt for food.

Tarantulas hunt insects and other small animals. These animals are called their *prey*.

Some spiders spin sticky webs to catch prey. But tarantulas don't. How do tarantulas get their food?

A hungry tarantula waits quietly inside its burrow or tube web.

When a small animal comes near, the tarantula attacks!

The tarantula bites the prey. Its fangs shoot *venom* into the prey. Venom is a kind of poison.

The venom keeps the prey
from moving.

Next, the tarantula spits juice into
the prey.

The juice makes the prey's insides mushy. The tarantula sucks out the mush.

Female tarantulas lay eggs. They put the eggs in a bag called an *egg sac*.

Baby tarantulas hatch out of the eggs.

The babies are called *spiderlings*.

Newly hatched spiderlings are tiny.
But they already know how to hunt
and eat prey.

A tarantula's exoskeleton can't stretch. So as the spiderling eats, its skin becomes too tight.

How can the baby tarantula grow?

The spiderling *molts*.

Inside its exoskeleton, a bigger skin forms. The exoskeleton splits open, and the spiderling crawls out.

The new skin is soft at first. But soon it becomes hard. It becomes a new, bigger exoskeleton.

After a while, the spiderling's
exoskeleton becomes tight again.
The young spider molts again.
It grows even bigger.

Soon it will be a grown-up tarantula.

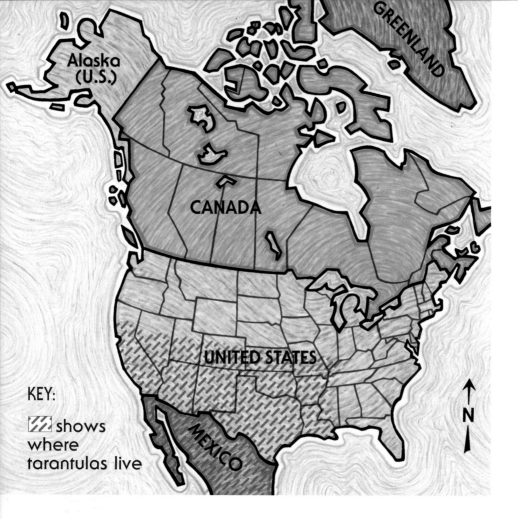

KEY:

▨ shows where tarantulas live

Alaska (U.S.)

GREENLAND

CANADA

UNITED STATES

MEXICO

N

Find your state or province on this map. Do tarantulas live near you?

Parts of a Tarantula's Body

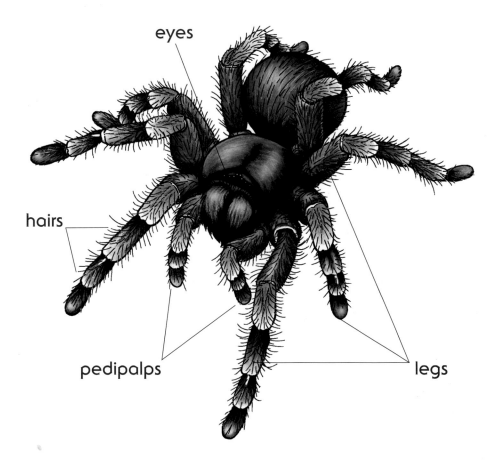

eyes

hairs

pedipalps

legs

Glossary

burrows: holes in the ground where tarantulas live

egg sac: the bag a female tarantula makes to hold her eggs

exoskeleton: a tarantula's hard, tough skin

molts: sheds its old skin. Tarantulas have to shed their skin so they can grow.

pedipalps: leglike "feelers" that a tarantula uses to hold its food

prey: the animals tarantulas hunt and eat

rain forests: forests that get a lot of rain each year

spiderlings: baby tarantulas

spiders: animals with eight legs and two main body parts

venom: a tarantula's poison

Further Reading and Websites

Berman, Ruth. *Spinning Spiders*. Minneapolis: Lerner Publications Company, 1998.

Glaser, Linda. *Spectacular Spiders*. Minneapolis: Millbrook Press, 1999.

DesertUSA—Tarantulas
http://www.desertusa.com/july96/du_taran.html

National Geographic—Tarantulas
http://www.nationalgeographic.com/tarantulas/index2.html

Index

Photo Acknowledgments

The photographs in this book are reproduced with the permission of:
© Mary Clay/Taxi/Getty Images, cover, p. 26; © Justin Sullivan/Getty
Images, p. 3; © JH Pete Carmichael/The Image Bank/Getty Images, p. 4;
© Wegner, P./Peter Arnold, Inc., pp. 5, 17, 18; © Joe McDonald/Visuals
Unlimited, pp. 6, 8; © age fotostock/SuperStock, p. 7; © Dorling
Kindersley/Getty Images, p. 9; © C. Allan Morgan/Peter Arnold, Inc., p. 10;
© Bruce Davidson/naturepl.com, p. 11; © Meul, J./Peter Arnold, Inc., p. 12;
© Mark Moffett/Minden Pictures, pp. 13, 20; © Royalty-Free/CORBIS, p. 14;
© Ian Waldie/Getty Images, p. 15; © Heidi and Hans-Jurgen
Koch/Minden Pictures, p. 16; © Claus Meyer/Minden Pictures, pp. 19, 27;
© Robert and Linda Mitchell, p. 21; © Gerald Moore, p. 22; © Gerry
Bishop/Visuals Unlimited, p. 23; © BIOS Lefévre Michel/Peter Arnold, Inc.,
p. 24; © Tom McHugh/Photo Researchers, Inc., p. 25.